Eye See Different

By LaToshia Handley Martin

A True Story of Resilience and Determination

Dedications

I dedicate this book to my mother, the late Margaret Ann Hall Handley. She never allowed me to feel sorry for myself. She supported me in all things and made sure that I had everything to be successful and live a normal life being legally blind.

I also dedicate this book to my children— my daughter, Toniya Handley, and my sons, Kenneth Martin, Jr., and Kai Martin.

Special Thanks

I want to thank three special people in my life for always believing in me and pushing me into my purpose. Words cannot begin to capture the gratitude for their love and continued support.

Kenneth Martin Sr, my husband

Dr. Calvin Moore Jr, my Pastor/Godbrother

Dr. Patrice J. Dawson, my best friend/sister

Table of Contents

Chapter

1

Nearsighted

Insight:

Do not be ashamed of how God made you. Be confident in who you are. Do not allow your flaws to hinder you from being great.

My name is LaToshia and I know you're probably looking at the title wondering what it means. Well, I would like to take you on a journey. On this journey you will need your natural eyes to follow, but your spiritual eyes to really understand where we are actually going. The eye is a part of the human body that has a lot of responsibilities. The eye is also one of the five senses that we have. We use our eyes to see. Point blank! We need our eyes to navigate our footsteps, sense of direction, decision-making, learning development and so much more. Our eyes are very sensitive and requires protective shields called eyelids. I know you didn't sign up for a science course, but I felt it necessary to help you understand how important our eyes really are.

I was in the fourth grade when I got my first pair of glasses. They were ugly! The frames were huge, and I hated them. I was nearsighted. I could see close up, but not far. I remember sitting in Mr. Snow's fourth grade class looking out of the window. I was able to see the street signs, car tags, and even the faces of people outside. This was impossible without my glasses. You would think that I would be excited about this, but I was not at all! I was embarrassed to wear them. Kids were just cruel back then. You were considered ugly, goofy or a nerd if you wore glasses. You were made fun of and laughed at. Me being shy and concerned about what others thought about me, I cried a lot and developed low self-esteem. This resulted in me not wearing my glasses all the time when I really needed them. I would take them on and off throughout the day. I even managed to see when people were and were not watching. They didn't have the cute glasses covered under my insurance plan, so I had to get what they covered. The ugly ones!

This only made things worse. Instead of me being grateful for what I had, I was mad. I felt like wearing glasses was a form of punishment. I decided to try and manipulate the situation. I would write big. I would sit in the front of the classroom. I did not like being up front, but I sat there. I liked to sit in the back because I was behind everybody, but I could not see back there unless I had on my glasses and that was not about to happen. I got older and was now in high school. I wanted to learn how to drive and I did. My mom let me practice in her car after I passed my driver's education class. I was only in the 9th grade when I took the class. It was only supposed to be taken by sophomores, juniors, or seniors. I tried to change my schedule but could not. I guess God knew his plans for my life. To top it all off I had finally gotten my contact lenses. Goodbye glasses! I thought! I kept getting those contacts stuck up in my eyelids, dropping them on the floor and losing them resulting in me half wearing them. When I did wear them, I had 2020 vision. It was on and popping. I thought I had arrived honey and hadn't even started yet! I saw the reason my mom was saying I was half sweeping, mopping and cleaning my mom's house. With those contacts on I can see all the dirt. I thought I was doing a good job until those two little lenses told me different. I would sometimes wear just one contact lens if I couldn't get the other one in. I felt that one good eye was better than two bad ones. This became real in my world of vision. Mom was letting me drive so I had a taste of freedom. Going places without my mother was exciting. My twin sister and I went on a lot of adventures until we took that trip.

Chapter

2

Blinded

In the summer of 1993, I attended Vacation Bible School, which lasted for a week. We usually went on a fun trip for participating. That year we went to White Waters Over Georgia water park. The trip was exclusive. We had a chartered bus with comfortable, reclining seats. As a teenager this was big! We had this luxury bus, but nowhere to eat our lunches. Being that we didn't reserve a pavilion and the park was so crowded with people , we had to eat our lunch on the bus. This was cool with us because while everybody else was sitting outside in the hot sun. We were chilling, relaxing and eating our lunch on an air- conditioned bus. When everyone had completed their meals, we went back into the water park. We had the time of our lives. In fact, I couldn't wait to go back again. The majority of us slept most of the way back home due to the drain from the sun and the motion of the water. When I got home, I was not feeling too good. I laid around a few days and I began to feel worse. My mother then took me to the emergency room. I was diagnosed with pneumonia, bronchitis and strep throat. I was sick as a dog. I was truly in bad shape. I couldn't keep my food down. It hurt me too vomit, so I stopped eating. I didn't have an appetite anymore. I had to force myself to take my medication with milk to prevent me from getting even sicker. I was sick the whole summer. That's bad news, right?! At the beginning of the summer I was driving and going on adventures and now I had to spend the rest of the summer in the bed. The doctors explained to us how this was possible and came about. Unfortunately, there was some bacteria that "escaped" the chlorine. He suggested someone might have defecated or urinated in the water. I was sick. One of the greatest trips of my life turned out to be one that left me with lifelong memories. Because it was such a gigantic park there was no way possible to locate or pinpoint where or when it happened. My mind went back to one of the rides called the toilet bowl flush where you go down this big slope and you end up in the commode then you spin around in a circle and then get out. Just to make a joke, maybe it happened there. Sometimes you have to laugh to keep from crying. The facts still remained—I was sick.

The crazy part is I love to travel. At first, I said that I was never ever going to go back so that park again. Well so far, I haven't. Sometimes we are so anxious to go places. Is that a bad thing? Absolutely not. All places are not good for us to go to or visit, including a waterpark. What is the harm in it? Who would have ever thought that this would happen? I know that I didn't. I often wonder how my life would have turned out if I had never taken that trip. I had never experienced being that sick before. I lost so much weight. I went to the school with my mom to pick up my sister from band practice some of my classmates thought that I was sick because I was pregnant. They were hilarious! I thought when you are pregnant you get bigger not smaller. I thought to myself, "Stay in school you fool" Oh sorry, that slipped. Listen 3 diagnosis, meds taken 3 times a day and lasting 30 days. The number three is my number. God deals with me in threes. Then I didn't value it, but because of the Trinity I rejoice. A lot of people die from pneumonia alone. As a child I didn't understand that fact. Let's keep moving.

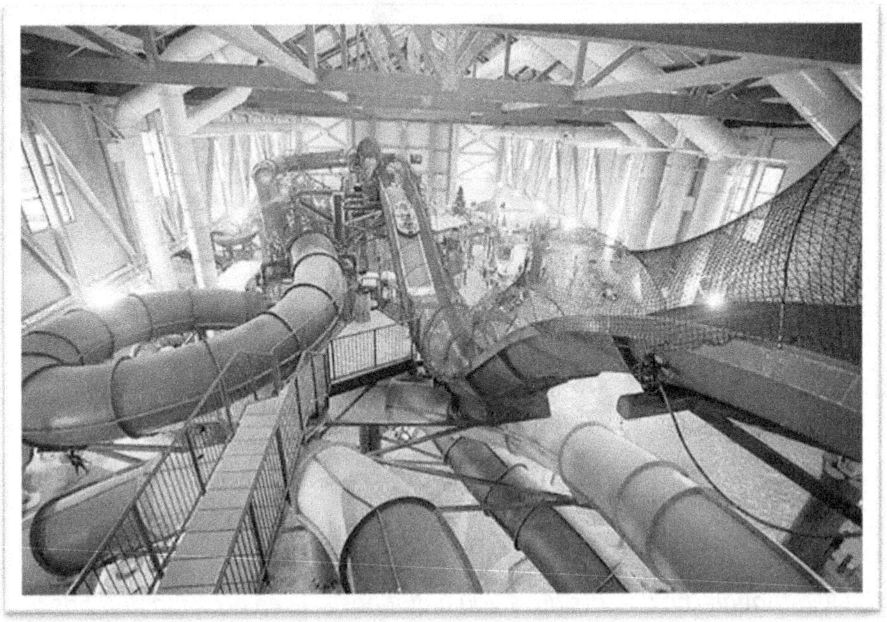

Chapter

3

The Diagnosis

At the end of recovery, I started to gain an appetite. I wanted some watermelon. One of my favorite fruits! I just had to have it! Have you ever wanted something so bad that you can already taste it in your mouth? Well, that's where I was at this moment. My taste buds were now alive again and they were revived and ready to attack. Well it was a lovely evening and I decided to go to the supermarket that was just a few blocks away from where we lived. My twin sister rode in the car with me. She didn't know how to drive so she sat in the passenger seat. We got in the car put on our seat belts and I started the engine. We took off up the hill. Maybe 2 minutes after departing I became blind. What do I mean blind? I could not see. I could see fine when I got in the car but when I pulled off, I could only see darkness and light. I immediately said to my sister that I couldn't see, and she didn't freak out she calmly responded with, "What do you mean you can't see?" I replied, "I can't see." I did not panic either which was surprising to me. I told her that she was going to have to help us get back home. She became my eyes. I control the gas and the brake pedals, and she controlled the steering wheel. We made it all the way back home safely. The strangest thing happened. There were no other cars on either road that we traveled on. Actually, I think it was all God. He was protecting us from dangers seen and unseen. He was right there with us the entire time. When we got home we rushed into the house to tell my mother what happened. She immediately took me to the emergency room, again. We were there for so many hours. The emergency room was crowded and most of all the seats were taken. I was so afraid. I didn't know what was going on. My mind was all over theplace.

First, I was sick the whole summer and now when I'm starting to actually feel better this happens. My life is over, I thought for a split second. Because I was raised in the church, I was introduced to God at an early age. I had a real relationship with him as a young child. Did it make me perfect? No! Did I make mistakes? Yes! Did I understand that He was in control of this situation? You better believe I did! No Doubt! Was I afraid? Absolutely, as a matter of fact I was terrified. I thought I was going to leave there with a prescription and a follow-up appointment with my primary physician and back to normal I'd go. Well unfortunately it didn't go as I thought it would. Oh, I had a follow-up appointment all right. I had several. I went from Doctor to Specialist and still no diagnosis. Then I was sent to the Eye Foundation. I was referred to Dr. Klein. He scoped the situation and diagnosed me with Optic Atrophy. What in the world is that? Well, it is an eye condition where the optic nerve slowly deteriorate and eventually results in total loss of vision. I'm telling you this now because I have become very knowledgeable of it as an adult but back then I had no clue what it was. I was all out of focus. All I know is that I had a glimpse of what 2020 Vision look like right before my site changed forever.

The doctors said that I would never see like I used to again. They were correct, but they were talking in the natural. They must not have yet tapped into the spiritual and neither did I at the time. They also recommended Rehabilitation. Rehab! What is life coming to for me? Is it over? I'm a child! Why do I have to go through this? This is too much! My mother listened to me, but she did not allow me to waddle in pity or defeat. She did what a great mother does and that's be strong when your children are weak. I acknowledge her strength so much because she had a situation of her own to deal with at that same time. She was diagnosed with breast cancer. After months of taking chemo, she still had to have one of her breasts removed. This operation left her disabled because she had limited usage of her arm which resulted in frozen shoulder syndrome. She had worked all her life. Now her life had changed forever. She could have been selfish and focused only on herself, but she did not. She was there for me every step of the way. She pressed through her pain and problems to encourage me. You know what? That is what mothers do. Mothers are strong and they fight, and they press through any situation and they protect their children no matter what.

If I had the choice of choosing a mother I would definitely choose mine. God knows who is fit for the job. My mom had some hang-ups in her past, but she became such a wonderful mother overall. I truly appreciated her and the things that she planted inside my spirit; as a mother myself. When I became a mother, she taught me so many things and one thing that I would never forget that she taught me was to be responsible. She also taught me that your children come first. Well, my mother and I became remarkably close friends during this time. We both were dealing with a midlife crisis. Well, I was not middle-aged at the time. Ha ha ha! We leaned on each other. She encouraged me and I encouraged her. This was a big pill to swallow. In fact, it was a horse pill! You never know which way life is going to turn but you have to accept what God allows and move forward and that is definitely what my mother and I did. All of this bonded us closer together. We really became ride or dies. We were inseparable. God has a way of getting our attention to make us grow up. Because I couldn't drive anymore my mom took me everywhere, even to Sunday School. I was a faithful Sunday School attendant and with that being a fact my mother became one as well. This was not only beneficial to me but beneficial to my mother's spiritual development. We often miss the mark in life, but I think that this was all in God's plan. When we get off the right road, He has a way of derailing us onto the

right path. What a mighty God we serve!

Chapter

4

Peripheral

Vision

Insight:

Use what you have to get the job done. That's what Jesus did. He used a little and performed a lot of big miracles. Remember if you trust Him something big will happen.

How do I adjust to this new life of sight? Where do I begin? What is Rehabilitation? I thought only substance abusers went there. I don't do any of that, so I'm lost here. Well, today in 2020, I Googled it. Rehabilitation is the action of restoring someone to health or normal life through training and therapy after impairment, addiction or illness. As I reflect on my rehabilitation journey it was just that. I remember Mr. Mike Jones, a totally blind white man. He was my first counselor from the center. He had a seeing eye dog. I was terrified of it because it was a dog and a huge one at that. They had to convince me that the dog would not harm me before I stepped foot in the auditorium where they waited for me. I believed them and went in to meet him. My first visit was at my school, Fairfield High School in Fairfield, Alabama. Everyone else thought it was cool seeing the dog there, but I didn't. However, when I became an adult, I wish that I had gotten a seeing eye dog, like Mr. Mike. I think maybe my life would have gone a little bit different and maybe I would not have made so many mistakes. Well, I can't do nothing about it now so- whatever! Mr. Mike was the first person from another race that I valued in my life. I don't know where he is today or whether if he is still alive but if he ever reads this book, I hope that he remembered me. With him in my life I started to believe in myself again. I had a lot of people fighting for me to recover. He arranged for me to go to the Alabama School for the Deaf and Blind. This place was so awesome. I met so many people from different backgrounds and races that were totally blind or deaf and they all had smiles on their faces. How in the world was I able to see that? Your guess is as good as mine, nevertheless, this surprised me. Now, if they can be happy and they couldn't see at all why shouldn't I be happy? They encouraged me. They spoke so very highly of me and made me feel like I was a part of a new family. There were several programs that they had available for me there. They specialized in helping disabled individuals to live as normal as possible. There was absolutely no room for self-pity or shame. I begin to believe in myself even more. Philippians 4:13 became my favorite scripture. "I can do all things through Christ which strengthens me." There is nothing that I can't do as long as I have God fighting for me and pushing me and allowing me to do it. Whenever someone told me that I couldn't do something I made it my business to prove them wrong. I would quote the scripture whenever I was faced with any challenge of any size. I know that folks did not expect for me to be able to do the things that I have done or the things that I am doing right now but it is all because of God and His unmerited favor over my life. Sometimes I would be around people that grew up with me and they would ask me questions about my sight or look at me out of the side of their eyes as if I were different from everybody else. Which I was, but why treat me that way?

Whenever someone is different people tend to look out of the corners of their eyes to disguise what they are thinking or actually doing. That person may not see you, but God does, and he is the ultimate judge. You know where you are today, but you don't know where you will be tomorrow. Don't look at people sideways or out of the corner of your eyes as a disgrace or to belittle them because you don't want that same energy to boomerang back to you. I was never a person that talked about others or try to make others feel bad, so I was covered on that end. I started to feel like I was going to be fine. I learned how to use a Mobility Cane, read Braille and how to use my ears, nose and hands to help me see. I also met Mr. Larson Turk, a black man that was totally blind. He was my second counselor. In his program I learned skills and techniques on how to live a normal life as a blind person in the household. Ms. Sue, one of his instructors, who was also totally blind, came to our house. She used bright color fabric paint to mark the stove, microwave, and oven. Drying as a raised bubble, the paint markings would soon serve as my indications for temperature controls and other operational provisions. Soon, I could feel those indications and know the temperatures, as well as operate the washing machine and dryer. I was also given large printed and safe tools like mittens for the oven, measuring tools and so much more. This was so extremely helpful. I was able to do more for myself. It was on now baby! My life was starting to feel normal again. Mr. Turk did everything in his power to help me. We had things in common. We both were singers and loved music. He was a musician as well. He had a studio in his home, and this blew my mind. This was so amazing to me. I became excited when I found out that a blind person could own and operate a music studio. That ignited a spark within me. How could someone with total vision loss, write, compose, publish, and record? I was curious to know if I could do something like that one day. Did I act upon it? Of course not! I was just trying to find my way. However, a few years later I started singing more frequently and developed a deep passion for it. I will be forever grateful for these people that God allowed to deposit so much love and encouragement that was so much needed in my life. The funny thing is that they say they learned a lot from me. I encouraged them as much as they encouraged me. I guess God knew what we all needed and who to get it from. Of course! He knows everything.

Being in high school I had to pass the Exit Exam. How was it going to be possible for me to do that if I couldn't read? At test time they brought a Close Captioned Television (CCTV) for me to take the test. I had never used one of those before that day. After a couple of hours, I was so sick. This machine magnifies the words so

I can see them myself. You have to move the tray back and forward, side to side and if your eyes are not used to it you will become dizzy and seasick. I was so upset. They took me to the office because they couldn't calm me down. I was an emotional wreck. I cried so hard in that office. I had so many dreams for my future and if I couldn't pass that test it was over. My computer teacher was there and witnessed it all. He took me into the hall to comfort me. He also shared with me how proud of me he was. He was one of the cute teachers that all of the students were crazy about. That made me feel better by itself. Mr. Turk came to my school shortly after that. They reached out to him to let him know what was going on and he came to see about me. He and his driver took me on a little field trip to the ice cream store and we relaxed and just talked. When we returned to the school, he told me how everyone that was in the office witnessing my meltdown was crying with me. He encouraged me to thank them for calling him to come and see about me and I did.

From this experience they made some arrangements to have a CCTV put in my computer classroom so that I can practice using the device throughout the school year. This will better prepare me for the next time to take the test. When test day came, I attacked it. I even finished before others. It took a while before the results came back. I was on the edge of my seat on the day to find out. I asked my English teacher Miss Shields if she had seen the results. She did. She told me that I passed. I screamed with so much joy in my heart to. She hugged me with tears in her eyes. She congratulated me and told me how proud she was. At the end of the day, I got my paper results. I had my sister to read them to me. I was then unstoppable. I was reassured that a form of blindness does not make you dumb or incapable of learning. I went on throughout high school with grace and confidence. I graduated with honors and a 3.4 grade point average. I received a full scholarship to Lawson State Community College. I maintained a 4.0 grade point average there, graduating with honors in Cosmetology. I loved to do hair and I still do hair today. Some people are amazed at how good I can do hair being partially blind; well seeing different. My answer is always, "it's only by the grace of God". I myself cannot explain how I am able to do the things that I can do but I give all glory and honor to God in heaven for the miracles signs and wonders here on earth. God never ceases to amaze me. I was so proud of myself. I learned how to use what I had to get the job done. That's my motto. I use my peripheral vision. From the side of my eyes I can see clearer, so I make it work for me. I was doing hair again and better than before. Be mindful that the doctor said that I would never live a normal life again. But God! I'm so glad that He is my primary physician! Guess what? He has the best coverage plans and the lowest rate. I only give him a dime out of earnings. My 10% activates his 90%

which equals 100% benefits. Do you need a referral? There is no line and no waiting. He is right there waiting for you at the door of your heart. Let Him in!

President's List Award

This is to certify that

LaToshia S. Handley

has been awarded special recognition for achieving
a perfect 4.0 grade point average
for the Fall Quarter 1997
at
Lawson State Community College
Birmingham, Alabama

January 8, 1998

Chapter

5

Magnified

Insight:
Don't look at people under your eye, cross-eyed, rolling your eyes, with your peripheral vision or with your eyes closed. The boomerang is real.

Do you remember the science lab, where we use magnifying glasses for research? I was introduced to advanced magnifiers for low vision. Hmmmm. This was interesting. I was always hoping for the day that I could read again fluently. In high school I used black permanent markers and so did my teachers. The smell gave me headaches. I was probably high too from the fumes! I had to use white typing paper instead of wide or college-ruled loose-leaf paper. I used one sheet of copy paper just to write one math problem for one question. I had to write it just that big in order for me to read it. I still had to strain my eyes to see with them. In 1999 I was at the rehab center and they were showing me new visual aids again. The instructor was interrupted by someone from her office. She had to read a document and stamp it. She took out a pair of glasses that had a plastic patch over one side and read the document. I was sitting right there so I saw it up close. I was curious to know what type of glasses they were so when she was done I asked her about them. She explained to me how to use them and that they were magnifying glasses. Afterwards I asked her if I could try them on. I couldn't believe what I was seeing. I could see so well. It was a miracle! I was able to read that paper so fluently. I didn't want to see anything else at this point. I knew these glasses were a game changer for me. They made me an appointment to go to the UAB School of Low Vision Rehabilitation so that I can get a pair of those glasses. I could hardly wait for that appointment. I got my glasses! I still have those glasses today and I use them every day. Unfortunately, they do not make them anymore, so I have to continue to repair these same glasses. I call them my miracle glasses. These glasses allow me to use my cell phone, read and write emails, and use apps and so much more. As a matter of fact, I used these glasses to write this book! I also received a mini telescope during this visit. It was so cute. It was so small that I could fit in my pocket or my pocketbook. I could use it to see far away distances. I used it at concerts, the movie theaters and sports events. I had it for a long time but unfortunately, I lost it. I wish I could get another one. I may just make another appointment at the Low Vision Clinic to see if they have come up with something new. I haven't been there in a while. Maybe it's time for me to go back!

Here's a nugget just for you. Everything is not what it seems. Take a closer look at that situation, thing or person from a different angle. Stop looking in the natural. Dissect it but don't blow it out of proportion. Just look deeper. We use magnifiers to see what the natural eye can't see. So, if you magnify God you will see what He sees and all that you have missed. Hopefully, you will get a better understanding and find a solution or even closure.

Okay, let's go back! I had these new glasses so now I'm ready to work. I had a job opportunity to work at a senior home or nursing home, but I chose neither. They wanted me to work on Sundays. This was out of the question! Well my church had a daycare and kindergarten and I decided to apply. I had my interview and was hired on the spot. It was so exciting to start a new adventure and chapter of my life. I was making my own money! I was hired as a teacher's aide but one year later I was promoted to be a K-2 Teacher, with my own classroom. This job was awesome! I loved it. I gave it my all. I would visit the daycare, as a child not knowing that my first real job would be there. My Aunt, Beverly Hall was a K-2 Teacher back then. I remember wrapping gifts for her students during Christmas time and yes, I did the same for my students. I must say that my aunt Miss Hall and others at the day care taught me very well. Mrs. Williams was the best director on the face of this earth. She did not treat me like a disabled individual. She pushed me into the excellent professional and humble teacher that I am today.

Unfortunately, Mrs. Williams retired and was replaced. All hell broke loose! I started to hate going to work because of the new director and the injustices I encountered. My skills and capabilities were minimized, and my disability was magnified. The new director did not give me a chance. She just came in the door with judgment. She took me before the board to change everything without facts. She always argued that I had to have an aide with me for the safety of the children. She felt like they were in danger with me alone. In my defense not one student got hurt on my watch before or after her being there. I knew my limits, so I operated accordingly. I stayed within my seeing range. If I had to leave the room, I'd leave them with a staff member, so they were never unattended. I was definitely on top of my game. She didn't even have a clue. I was cool with an aide. That meant less work for me. There was another co-worker there with a disability, as well. One of the most talented, hard-working, kind- hearted and humble women I know. She was deaf. This did not stop her from being one of the greatest teachers there. She made sure that she was prepared for each day and implemented crafts and entertainment for her students. I had a great respect for her, and she taught me some things too. We both ended up with aides in our classrooms. For years neither one of us had an aide, but we didn't mind. We always continued to give our best. We stood with integrity. You must be careful how you treat people because you never know when, where, or how it will come back to you. As for the director, she was dealt a bad hand of cards. That same board of directors treated her worse than she treated me. She was watched like a hawk every day. She was made to feel like she was incapable of doing her job without supervision. Sounds familiar to me. For all the days that I cried she cried more. For every pain that I felt in my heart, she felt more. This experience humbled her. She came to me and apologized. She expressed how proud she was of my work to my mother and me.

Chapter

6

Close Captured

Insight:
A closer look allows you to capture details, authenticity and value of someone or something.

There is an online meeting platform called Zoom. I use it for many purposes, such as my virtual preschool, Let's Fly Live Talk Show interviews, Songbird Ministries singers' rehearsals and Agape Praise Team rehearsals. (That was an advertising commercial line.) This platform gives up close and in personal experiences on a screen. My CCTV does the same, but it's not hooked up to the internet. After a long period of time, I found myself needing to take a closer look at myself. I was legally blind. Yes, but does that mean I was exempt from trials and making bad decisions? No. I dealt with so many hard times and obstacles that were designed to kill my character and purpose. I didn't know my purpose. What is purpose? Purpose is the reason for which something is done or created or for which something exists. We are God's creation, and he has a purpose for our lives. When we become believers in God, we begin to develop a relationship with him. When we focus in on His word, we capture His grace, favor, stability, power and so much more. Even with my glasses it takes a long time to read books. I downloaded the Bible app to read to me. This helps me tremendously. It erased all the excuses I had for not reading the Bible. No one has an excuse now, but many are given. As I explored the app, I learned so much and understood better. The Bible is actually very interesting and entertaining. You won't know that, if you don't read it or click on the app.

The more you know the more accountable you become. Some people stay away from the Bible for that reason. To me that is very pathetic and immature. When you are close to God you grow up. You put away childish thinking and doing. Maturity is essential to adulthood. You can be 50 years old and act like a child. A double-minded man or woman is unstable in all of their ways. When you are mature, you make better decisions and choices. You also have to be mindful of how you respond to other people's actions. I had people throughout the years say harmful things to me. Are you still blind? Can you see me? You still can't see? I showed maturity by not responding, but on the inside, I was crying like a baby. How can people be so cruel? People would leave me out, not invite me to functions, not speak to me knowing that I can't see them and worse. Yes, it hurts like hell, but I had to endure it. We can't control what others do or say, but we can control our responses. People tend to look at disabled individuals as outcasts, but that's who God uses. My pastor calls them misfits. I didn't fit into the crowd and you did not either. Only a person with purpose would even read a book like this and get this far. There is purpose in you reading this book and I believe it is to reassure to you that God can use anybody to do the work of His kingdom. Oh yeah! He has chosen you! Sorry to burst your little bubble, but God has called you for such a time as this. You know what you feel. Just do it. Walk through it. You are not in this alone. If he brings you to it, He will bring you through it. Take a close look at your life. Put the pieces together with his guidance and help. Allow him to lead you. Let him speak for you, to you and through you. Surrender to his will and lay yours aside. I am not telling you something that I haven't had to do myself. I had to do all of this and more. I no longer wonder if I can do anything anymore. I only trust God and wonder what He's going to allow me to do next. Selah.

Chapter

7

Opening My Spiritual Eyes

Insight:
If you can see in the spirit, you have been set aside by God. Treasure the gifts that God gives you and use them so that only he can be glorified.

Have you ever heard someone mention seeing in the spirit? Well, as a young adult I had not, but as I approached my late twenties I did. This was something new to me since I grew up in a traditional church. I never remembered something like this being taught or even discussed unless Elder Moore, an associate minister at the church said it. He was pretty much the only one at my church that ever brought it up. That little bit tickled my interest. I have the ability to see things before they're done and hear things before, they're said. How is this possible? I see things in the Spirit, supernatural and through the eyes of the Holy Spirit. I have always been able to do this, but never fully understood why or what was going on. I was tripping because how can I see these things and I'm partially blind in both of my eyes? My left eye is worse than my right eye. If I close my right eye I can't function well. I most definitely will need assistance. If I close my left eye I am still in the game. This was crazy to me. It's so real. When I started noticing and tracking it, it literally almost tripped me out. I was sitting on the toilet chilling. My legs were propped open on the tub that was in front of me. I had my cell phone in my hand. I saw my cell phone fall out of my hand and into the toilet. This was not actually happening. It was a vision. I closed my legs and continued to look at my phone. Well, a few minutes later my cell phone slipped out of my hands and fell onto my lap. I was in shock. At this time, I started to monitor and pay more attention when things like this happened to me. I was told that they were visions. In other words, seeing in the spirit. Does this mean or make me a prophet or a spiritual advisor? Can I now read palms or tell you your future? Most definitely not! I am not a witch or a psychic. Some people get it twisted. God can use you for a time or two, to get his message across. That does not mean that you are a prophet. I think God gave me those gifts so that He would be glorified and that I would believe. Anytime someone asks me questions like: *How did you see that? I didn't see that so, how did you?* My answer is always, "ask God, because I don't know!" I remember a little while after being diagnosed, God allowed me to see a tiny spider crawling on my bed. I remember being in the car with my best friend, Patrice, and telling her to stop her car because she was too close to the car in front of us. She would have hit it if I had not said anything. I often reflect on how I can direct someone in a vehicle to get to and from different locations. How can I do these things? Nobody, but God! I can have a plate of food in my face and not know what was on it unless I fixed it myself. When taking pictures, I ask to make sure my eyes are straight and focused. The only way I can watch TV is if I am sitting or standing directly in front of it. I am glad that they made tablets or otherwise I would just have to listen to it. If I look into the mirror I can't see myself. I have to get one foot or less close to it to see. I can't apply makeup or polish my own nails either. If I haven't seen you in a while I wouldn't have known that it was you unless I recognize your voice. People that are close to me and understand that my situation is real, they will identify themselves while approaching me or call my name so that I can hear their voices. If I am with someone at an unfamiliar place they will direct me up or downstairs. I thank God for those people. I do understand that some people forget that I am this way because I sometimes forget. I function well and if you don't know it is sometimes hard to notice it. I've kind of mastered it. Being that I don't want to be treated differently than others, I uniquely control my situation. I remember walking to and from schools or stores, basically anywhere that I need to go. Sometimes I would walk by myself or my daughter Toniya would be with me. I bet you are wondering why am I walking? Well, when you are disabled you have to wait until someone's schedule is free to take you somewhere. I can't make someone stop what they're doing to accommodate me so I walked or rode the city bus. It was heartbreaking at times because I couldn't depend on some of my family members to help me, but then God always sent someone to help me. He protected us when we walked or rode the bus. I have adjusted well to seeing naturally and spiritually. All of it keeps me believing in the power and favor of God. I get frustrated sometimes, but I continue to press forward. I think seeing in the spirit is a gift that only God can give. Just think with these natural eyes I can see strictly what God wants me to see. The gift of seeing in the spirit allows me to see what God sees. The gift was always there but my life and lifestyle had to line up with His will so that my spiritual eyes could be opened. All visions aren't good and positive. I've seen people in caskets. I've seen car wrecks in the spirit. When these things happen, I thank God for His angels and protection. God's will is going to be done whether we like it or not.

Chapter

8

Because I see

Different

Insight:
Seeing is half the battle. Believing in someone whom you have never seen is the key to eternal life. It doesn't matter what you can or can't see in the natural. Allow God to show you things in the spirit realm so that miracles, signs and wonders can be manifested in the earth rim. He sees you.

We have power in what we say. Stop saying things that are contrary to what God says. I had a habit of saying that I can't see. I'm legally blind. I'm visually impaired. I amplified my diagnoses instead of magnifying my testimony. One day my sister in Christ, Kenyardia, told me to stop saying that I can't. You just see different she said. That blessed my soul. I never thought about it like that before she said that. I do see different! This was so profound. Now you know who inspired my book title. You never know what you speak into a person's life can affect them. In this case it changed my whole outlook on my situation. I say it all the time now. I see different! God allowed me to be so creative and gifted because I couldn't see. He did it because he made me to see different. My mother thought my condition was due to the sins that she committed in her life, but the Holy Spirit told me that it was not true. God allowed this to happen so that He would be glorified. Whenever people see the great works, He allows me to do He will be glorified because this is what He has ordained for my life. I had talents and gifts before I started seeing different. I am an artist in crafts and designs. I am a gospel recording artist. I am a poet, play writer and songwriter. I am an author. I am a licensed natural hair stylist. I am the founder and instructor of My Virtual Preschool online. The list goes on and on so make sure to read my author's page at the end of the book. God keeps adding to the list. You can do all things through Christ who gives you strength. All things are possible with God.

Never allow the enemy to trick you out of your destiny. Don't ever let people, strangers, family or friends keep you from receiving God's blessings. God has promised us life in abundance. If you don't want yours, I'll gladly take it. My sister Patrice said, if you give up everything you can have it all. I want all that God has for me. With that being said I proudly accept what God allowed in His will for me to experience because it didn't kill me. It built me into a dynamic soldier for Christ. I take full responsibility for my assignments that He places before me. I decree and declare that the year 2020 has really been a blessing to me. I was told by God years ago that 2020 was going to be a dynamic, unforgettable and miraculous year. It has been thus far. It's not over; He still has time! I was hoping that in the year of 2020 I would receive a miracle of my natural vision being restored and renewed. God has given me a new pair of eyes. I can see clearly in the spirit. If He chooses never to restore my natural vision, I'm satisfied. He didn't have to let me see as much as I do now. He has made lie out of the doctors. Every time I get my eyes checked, they say that nothing has changed and there is no progress. Everything is still the same. Well they can't see what I see.

I can actually see clearer and better than when I was first diagnosed. They dilate my eyes to get a very close look, but they still don't see what God sees for me. Whose report will you believe? I choose God, Jesus and the Holy Spirit! I'm just waiting to see what's next. His plans are not our plans and He know the plans that He has for us. Well, I see different. What's your story? See you later!

Author Contact Page

LaToshia Handley Martin
Songbird Ministries
(Gospel Recording Artist)
Website: www.lhmsongbird.com
Email: lhsongbird36@gmail.com
Phone: (205) 225-9711

Let's Fly Live (Talk Show on YouTube)
Email: letsflylive@gmail.com
My Virtual Preschool (Zoom Classroom for ages 18mo.-4 yrs)
Email: myvirtualpreschooler@gmail.com
Connect and Follow us on Facebook and Subscribe to YouTube Channel!

Purchase these products on Amazon or any digital outlet:

Built for This Album by LaToshia Handley Martin

God Its You Single by LaToshia Handley Martin

When A Rose Blooms Novella by LaToshia Handley Martin

Upcoming Album ***Authentic Worship*** by LaToshia Handley Martin will release in 2021!

About the Author

LaToshia Handley Martin, an African American woman and proud wife of Kenneth Martin, Sr. She is the mother of three beautiful children—her oldest, a daughter, Toniya; two sons Kenneth Jr (KJ) and Kai. She is also the guardian of her nephew Mariye Lee.

LaToshia loves her family very much and understands the importance of family. LaToshia is the founder of Songbird Ministries and is now a gospel recording artist. She is an author and songwriter. She enjoys writing poems, skits and plays. She is the founder and host on her talk show, Let's Fly Live, where she uses this platform to inspire and promote others. It airs on Sundays at 3 p.m. CST on YouTube. LaToshia is the founder and instructor at My Virtual Preschool on Zoom. She is also the Minister of Music at Agape Ministries, Inc., where she is also the

Director of Christian Education. She is currently a student at Agape Bible College for Pastoral Studies. At the age of 15, LaToshia was diagnosed with Optic Atrophy, resulting in impaired vision. With this condition there are limitations in sight. As you can see and read her accomplishments above it did not affect or limit her capabilities of prospering. God has allowed and used her mightily in the Earth. She believes that she can do all things through Christ which strengthens her and that there are no limits with God. This book was written to encourage her children and others. She wants everyone to know how great and powerful God is and that He will use you and your short comings to bless you and most of all, glorify Him!